Increased

Sales

God's Way!

By L.M. Keatts

Copyright © 2015 by L.M. Keatts

Author's Note

Before you go out and spend a good penny on books, CD's, DVD's, Computer programs, Workshops, Seminars and even pulling your hair out in the process of doing everything, keep reading!

Did you know that you can have the same success in sales as those that you read about? In fact, if you will read this book with paper and pen you will far exceed all the rest.

I had just gotten hired by a company that did business on a daily basis with the Costco Wholesale Stores around the United States. It was my very first day and no one really expects very much out of you on that first day. Costco used an outside company to sell their products. The sales Advisors were assigned daily certain Costco items to sell and you never got to choose the products. In fact, you had to hit the floor with your product and had very little time in preparation!

That first day I sold approximately 85 boxes of breakfast snack crackers. My sales were higher on that first day than anyone else!

How did I accomplish that amount of sales on my first day?

People are successful because they prepare to be successful. In this book I'm going to teach you not only how to be successful as a sales person but how to stay successful as a sales person. Anyone can sell. But can you keep those numbers on a regular basis?

This book is not just for the seasoned sales person that wants to be better it is for anyone that wants to be better. There's room in all of us for improvement.

In every one of us there is a potential for success. But knowing that you have it is not enough. You have to tap into it. In this book I will teach you the keys to tapping into your God given potentials. By doing so, you will learn how to market yourself and understand the true science of selling.

-L.M. Keatts

To my best friend, my wife

Introduction

Many years ago I penned, "To be an accomplished teacher is to be an applied student." To be an accomplished anything in life, even sales you have to first be a student of sales but not just a student, an applied student. It is a known fact that anything you put yourself into the most is exactly what you're going to get out of it. I was talking to my son the other night in my office and I went over some of these same things. Mediocrity is generally what the world chases after for the most part because it doesn't require you to do very much. Not having the right ingredients will sour your task. There are men and women with Fortune 500 sales that couldn't care less how they got it.

It isn't a prerequisite to being successful in sales to do it God's way but it is a prerequisite in having record high sales every day!

For Example:

You just got a promotion at work as a Sales Manager. Your new position allows you some much needed time for your family. As the new sales manager you are in charge of company training. Also, without your knowledge your company has decided to celebrate your success. On the way home from the office you pull the car off the road and turn the engine off. You get home fifteen minutes late because during that time you were praising God.

Six months later you're promoted again. You're still a training manager but now you're traveling around the United States as a regional training manager!

- A number of years ago I read about those at Enron. This would be a Fortune 500 company. But something went very wrong in that operation. What eventually happened? The company had a collapse.

- When I was a kid I heard a very sad story of a man that had acquired much wealth in his business but because he didn't follow certain principles his company folded. He went from being a millionaire to having problems paying his light bill!

You need to do more to stay afloat in business if you want to end the day good.

In 2013, God spoke to my heart about the application of Ten Principles. He began to touch on certain things that I had missed in my business and where a lot of people miss it as well. Even some Christians!

I'm not going to draw this book out and make it real long to read. I think sometimes people make things rather complicated. If you are satisfied with your sales numbers then you wasted your money buying my book.

- This book is for those that are sick and tired of the norm in their sales and want to start kicking it up a notch.

- This book is for those that want to be promoted the next day not some day

- This book is for those that want to become a part of the Who's Who in sales in America.

In this book there are ten key principles that I really want you to look at. Now you were probably just thinking, "Let's look at them." But sometimes there are other issues that we have to measure first. For example, Many times someone can't move forward in their life and business because there are things in the way. Let me ask you a question: How is your relationship with God or do you even have one for that matter?

Did you know that everything pivots around our relationship with God?

While in prison many years ago, I was reading the Bible and I came across **Psalm 68:6.** In this verse of scripture God revealed a key to me that will unlock the door in your business!

"God gives the desolate a home to dwell in; he leads out the prisoners to prosperity; but the rebellious dwell in a parched land." (RSV)

I asked the Holy Spirit to give me insight into what I was reading. A parched land is a place where nothing goes right.

Perhaps you feel like you are up against a wall in your business. You have pulled out the books and even brought in someone else to help you. But for some reason you feel like you're between a rock and hard place!

Your land is parched. Your land is the life that has been assigned to you.

Let me ask you a question: What is the opposite of a parched land? We need to find the Answer before we can move on. Another word for parched is dry. The Holy Spirit also revealed it to me. The opposite of a parched or dry land is a land that is well water!

Let me ask you a question: Are you living in a dry land or a well watered land?

There are consequences for rejecting God in your life. When God is not in the center of your marriage what usually happens? You make bad decisions along the way and before you even realize it your marriage is gone.

What happens when you leave God out of your business affairs? You make improper decisions and your business drowns.

Your reason for rejecting God all of your life or some of it really matters not. The only thing that matters to God is your **immediate decision** to turn back to Him with your whole heart and turn every area of your life over to Him. So are you ready to step into a life that you could **never** have on your own?

Prayer:

"Father God I come before you in the name of Jesus. Father, I have really messed up in my own life. I have not put you first. I have really kept you out of my life. Father, the Bible says in Romans 10:13, that if I call on the name of the Lord I shall be saved. I'm calling on you now. I need you. And I ask you to take over my life right now. Everything that I have messed up I ask you to fix." Amen

First Principle:

Recognizing that every ounce of ability comes from God will put you on the road to success.

I don't care what school you attended or how intelligent you are. Every fiber of who you are came from God. I don't care what science tries to tell you, your abilities came from God. You inherited your intelligence from Him. You were hand pick and gifted before you were born! The key to having total success in business rest's completely in this knowledge.

Having a good week in your sales and having a bad week is up to you. If you will put Him first in your work place you will see a turnaround almost instantly!

How do you accomplish that?

I'm going guide you through the process. I'm going to give you some tools that will assist you in doing it for yourself. I want you to look at two scenarios.

- You just got hired for a company as their operations manager. As an OM your work detail is writing proposals and securing contracts. You're a closer and you're good at what you do. Your sales are up. After work there's a little office get together to compare weekly sales and guess what? You're now the new honcho. Your success has paid off financially and socially. You begin after a while to act smug around the office and now no one even wants to be around you. You give yourself the credit and two weeks later your sales drop by 98 percent!

- You realize that there are always opportunities to brag about yourself and act smug around others. You choose not follow down this path and give all of the credit to God. When your co-workers pat you on the back for a job well down you ignore the gesture and continue to be mindful that it is God that had open all of doors in your life!

If you are dissatisfied with your numbers you can make a change right now. The key ingredient here is in your **attitude.** Recognize right now that everything up to this point is all you're doing. Your low sales numbers is a direct result of the way you have done things. I want you to know that the devil has sabotaged your success up to this point. But from this day on he will not be able to move forward in your business. **If you keep your eyes on God and stay focused**.

Second Principle:

"Never start out your day without prayer and making confessions of faith of who you are as a Christian".

I can't even tell you how many times that I left my home without first thanking God for another day much less anything else!

My pastor is really good with this. The moment his eyes open he is praising God for another day. Driving down the road he is talking to God!

Now that you have made some changes in your life you have a right to believe God for better things. For the most part you have been living on the edge so to speak. You have been living for yourself only. The Bible calls a person like this a child of the devil. There are children of the devil in all walks of life. These people go day in and day out living like beggars. Not having enough or having too much and not having the wisdom to maintain what they have.

When you asked God to fix what you messed up, right then you became a child of God! And I want to assure you that there is absolutely no one that wants you to succeed more than God does. Look at what **Proverbs 16:21** has to say,

"Death and life are in the power of the tongue..."

Do you even realize that you control what happens next in your life?

The word death means to execute. In this sense of the word we are referring to something that is annihilated, to nullify.

When you speak negative words over your situation you are bringing to death anything good that could ever happen to you. **You are stopping the process.**

Death and Life are in the power of the **tongue.** The Bible declares this to be true.

So my question is: What have you been speaking over your life? **Give it some serious thought.**

Let's take a look at two examples that I believe will help you to understand.

- Jim is basically a good employee according to **his** standards. For five years now he has been passed over for a promotion in the company. Jim on many occasions often gets to work early and stays late but when the promotions are handed out his hand is empty! On Friday's after work some of the fellows get together and always Jim never grows tired of unloading on his co-workers complaint after complaint.

What do you think Jim is doing? By the words that he is speaking out of his mouth, complaint after complaint, Jim is **sabotaging** himself.

Negative words are words of death. They literally will kill your chance for success.

- **I'm not smart enough**
- **I'm too old**
- **They don't like me**
- **They're never going to promote me**
- **They will probably just pass me over**
- **I'm not like John, I could never be a salesman like him**
- **I'm not like Susan, I could never be a sales woman like her**

Author's Note:

- I remember once when I was up for a promotion that I got passed over and it was my fault. That morning before the interview everything out of my mouth was defeat. "They're probably going to give it to someone else." And guess what? They did exactly what I said. Again, look at **Proverbs 18:21.**

Death and life

Are in the power of the tongue!

What you speak out of your mouth good or bad will put you over or bring you down.

- Robert has worked for Bridge-Mark for only six months. His position at the company according to most is not very appealing, Robert is a janitor. Most people would turn their noses up at such a job. Robert understands that even a job like that of a janitor is a blessing. Robert understands that jobs of any kind are far in between and he is blessed just to have a job. There is never a day that ends on an empty note. Boarding the bus, Robert walks to the back and quietly whispers," Thank you for my job."

Eight days later the shift supervisor calls Robert into her office. Because of Robert's integrity on the job he gets a fifty cent raise and promoted to floor supervisor! He had only been there for six months but in that small time frame he performed better than anyone in his department and he got rewarded for it.

If you want things to change you have to **Make** a change. To change your circumstances you're going to have to change your language starting right now!

Third Principle:

"Recognizing the fact that God is the one that causes the sale through the skills he has instilled in you and brings the success through the closing process."

My quick prayer for you:

Father, for the person reading this book I ask you to reveal the third principle to them, In Jesus Name. Amen.

- On my first day at Costco I mentioned to you that I had sold approximately 85 boxes of Breakfast Snack

Crackers. Roughly we are talking about $600.00.

This third principle is so tedious that I want to spend some time on it with you. If you are like me sometimes it takes a while before it literally sinks in! Don't let anyone tell you that Writer's and Author's are brilliant people. Personally, I think just the opposite.

If you are selling a Vacuum door to door and at the end of the day your numbers are pass your quota and tomorrow even better, who gets the credit?

- I once read a book by a former attorney that ended up in prison but while there he gave his life to God. After his release from prison he couldn't get much work due to his criminal record so he took a job selling ice cream. This man gave God the credit for his sales every day. Do you want to know what happened? His sales hit the roof so to speak!

Recognize that it is God that is causing people to purchase your product.

- You're out selling Vacuum Cleaners. As you approach one of the houses suddenly the front light goes out! The lady that lives there has no intention of buying anything that you are selling. But for some reason she opens the door and allows you to do a demonstration. She listens but that's as far as she will go. As you get up to leave she has a change of heart!

This lady is usually very rude to sales people. In fact, she has never let anyone in her house!

You made a sale. Who gets the credit?

Recognize that it is God doing it and **(not you)** He is the one that brought you the sale, but how?

Where did you get your skills? Do you want the answer? **God**

- **Recognizing** that it is God that brings the sale.
- **Recognizing** that it is God that gave you a potential to sell.

1. When you profit, God gets the credit.

This is sometimes very hard to do because as humans we want the credit. God has another way that will bring increased sales!

- **Do you want your sales to double?**
- **Do you want your sales to multiple?**
- **Or do you want them to stay the same?**

Let me ask you a question:

When are you going to get tired of living a mundane life?

I hear in the news the politicians campaigning to make America great again. I think we need to make the Sales Person great again!

The 1940's brought in a great era for the American sales person. Years ago workers took great pride in the way they looked. Today we work for different reasons.

When I was in sales for a company did business for Costco and I might also state here a very good company, a couple of the sales persons were only there for a pay check. You could clearly see this in their demeanor. If you are in sales, get excited about what you are doing. Let me give you a rule of thumb. If you will get excited about your job, the customer will follow and you will close the deal!

Forth Principle

"Never give exaggerated information about the product you are selling."

- Jerry just got hired at a cell phone store and a part of his duties is to work the front counter. Jerry has been on the job one week now and has only sold two phones. Instead of believing that things will get better he devises a plan for better sales.

  Right before his shift is over a customer walks in the store. She's looking for a certain type of phone that Jerry absolutely knows nothing about. In the process of making the sale Jerry tells the customer that the phone has a special device that will switch from a 3G to a 4G to increase the capacity. However, this isn't true. In fact, this isn't true for any cell phone.

Note: Giving exaggerated information to a customer might come back and bite you so to speak. So don't do it.

Fifth Principle:

"The more you know about the product you are selling the more your sales will be."

The company that employed me at Costco hired me as a Sales Advisor. I was to promote and sell certain items. My time for preparation was approximately 30 minutes after I arrived! What do you do in so short of a time?

Instead of getting all bent out of shape and giving up I decided to locate key factors about the product. If I was selling food items I would study the Nutrition Facts. This usually gave me the edge that I needed in closing the sale.

This applies to sales persons on every type of avenue. Never be unprepared. It will cost you a sale. Customers usually know when the sales person is knowledgeable and when they are not. Again, let me highly encourage you to take the time to know all you can about the product you are selling. It can literally make the difference whether you close the sale or not!

Sixth Principle:

"The customer's first impression of you the sales person is up to you."

Did you know that?

You only get one opportunity to sell yourself with each customer! After they walk away that's it. How you market yourself with each customer will greatly affect your sales, good or bad.

How others perceive you is very important. It doesn't matter what your station in life is. Whether you sell stocks on Wall Street or shine shoes in New York your customers need to have a good impression of you. And it rest entirely on your shoulders.

There are three things that customers look at.

1. Your finger nails
2. Your shoes
3. Your breath

I have seen sales persons with dirty finger nails. If you have to change your tire on the way to work please wash your hands before clocking in.

If your shoes are dirty, take the time to wipe them off. If your shoes are worn out, purchase a new pair.

If you're breath could eat the rust off an old car, see a dentist!

How people perceive you is how they will receive you. Being professional is more than the money you earn. Being professional is also in looking professional!

Taking care of your appearance is the first step in the customer's first impression of you the sales person.

Seventh Principle:

"Do not be overly talkative about the product you are selling."

I can't begin to tell you how many times I blew a sale because of my big mouth! **Talking too much is talking too much.** Did you get that?

If you have to talk too much about the product you are selling then you probably

don't know too much about it. **The less you say will save you in the end!**

Some companies use scripts and sale pitches and that works sometimes but for the most part it doesn't.

Customers know when a sales person is using a script or throwing a sales pitch at them. If you will take the time to **prepare** yourself everyday **God's Way** then you will not need a sales script!

Eighth Principle:

"Remember, your customers best interest should always be your top priority."

"Mike was hired by a Nutrition company to promote and demonstrate. Today, Mike is baking some of the best tasting Garlic Bread around!

An elderly couple is very impressed and this gives Mike the perfect opportunity to make a sale for his company. Mike takes a moment to relax some and make small talk with his "new found friends". The husband and wife agree that the bread smells delicious. But they also mention that due to his condition of being a diabetic he wouldn't be able to sample or purchase any. Mike decides that making a sale is more important than the man's health.

Mike convinces the couple that garlic bread is really good for diabetic patients. Mike exaggerates and manipulates just to make a sale!"

Mike's top priority was greed not his elderly customers.

"The Art and Science of Selling" was a book published in 1922 by the National Salesmen's Training Association.

Salesmen in the early part of the last century were explicit. They were professional not only in their attire but as well in their demeanor.

God has a method for your success, **His way!**

No one respects a sales person that has only one agenda, their own.

If you want to see a sudden change in your sales then you are going to have to **MAKE** a sudden change in your motives!

Ninth Principle:

Satisfied customers always return to the same sales person."

You better believe that is the truth every single time.

Again, it goes back to that first impression of you. From the moment the customer walks up to the time they walk away they are reading you like a book! You only get one opportunity to market yourself.

1. Be honest about what you are trying to sale.

2. Do less talking and allow the customer to ask questions.

If you don't concern yourself with their needs some other sales person will.

Following this rule of thumb will gain you not just a customer but a valued friend!

Tenth Principle:

"One of the most important, treat each customer as you would a valued friend."

Appling the tenth principle in your sales will take you over the top!

Let me leave you with a thought to ponder:

IF YOUR CUSTOMER WAS GOD, HOW WOULD YOU TREAT HIM?

Books by L.M. Keatts

Laura's Diary

Washington's Diary

The Memoirs of Laura Ann Eddy

Increased Sales, God's Way

About the Author

L.M. Keatts is the President and Founder of the Independent Christian Writer's Association and is the author of four books on Amazon. Mr. Keatts holds a Ministerial License and an Ordination from Full Gospel Evangelistic Association and is a degree student at Anchor Theological Seminary & Bible Institute in Pharr Texas. The author resides in Mission Texas with his wife and step-son.

www.ingramcontent.com/pod-product-compliance
Lightning Source LLC
Chambersburg PA
CBHW071600170526
45166CB00004B/1731